DUXBURY BAY

Town Landing

Duxbury Yacht Club

Mrs Henry Wadsworth

"ACACIA VILLA"

A. E. Walker

Fannie Davenport Est.

Gamaliel Wadsworth

St. Margaret Hospital

E. P. Wadsworth

Mrs. L. Marsh Est.

Levi H. Cushing

HARDEN HILL

E. J. Smith

T. P. Freeman

Abbie R. S. Richards

Mrs. G. M. Winslow

Mrs. R. Holmes

Geo. L. Higgins

Wm Seymour

A. E. Walker

G. H. Stearns

E. M. Wadsworth (Res)

E. P. Wadsworth (Res)

John Josselyn

Clarence M. Taylor

Joseph Soule

W. H. Weston

W. J. Hastings

F. O. Crocker

Sophia Bradford

SQ. STATION

Mrs. T. C. Rogers

Mrs. T. C. Rogers

Freeman

Harrison Wadsworth

LINKS

H. J. Reynolds

Hiram Delano

SURPLUS ST.

THREE TREES

Louise G. Coburn

Seth Weston

Hamilton Wadsworth

G. A. Delano

N. Y. N. H. & H. R. R. Co.

DIV.

The NATHAN BREWSTER PLACE

O. A. Symmes

Town of Duxbury

G. M. Weston

Mrs. K. Faye

DEPOT

Hunt & Rich

SOUTH DUXBURY STATION

John Josselyn

Plym Nail Bank

Jas Mackay

Mrs. C. Foster

Mrs. Lewis

Fred Sherman

HALLS

DEPOT ST.

SOUTH DUXBURY P. O.

SCHOOL

STANDISH

CORNER

Ann T. Winsor

Pilgrim Ck.

Geo W. Winsor

SCHOOLS

Duxbury...
PAST & PRESENT

Patrick T. J. Browne
Norman R. Forgit

Published by the

Duxbury Rural & Historical Society, Inc.

479 Washington Street, P.O. Box 2865
Duxbury, Massachusetts 02331
781-934-6106; Fax 781-934-5730
www.duxburyhistory.org

Duxbury Rural & Historical Society Publications Committee

William McArdle, *Chairman*
Jayne Talmage, *Secretary*
Patrick Browne
Norman R. Forgit
Katherine H. Pillsbury
Alice Vautrain

Design & Production

Norman R. Forgit

Printing

John P. Pow Co., Inc., Boston

Printed in the United States of America

ISBN-10: 0-941859-11-8
ISBN-13: 978-0-941859-11-0

First Edition

Preface

Change and endurance. These are the two dichotomous themes that emerged as this publication began to take shape.

Even before we embarked on this project, we knew that there is something uniquely compelling about viewing historical photographs in a "past and present" format. To see landscapes as they appeared 100 years ago together with the same scene today allows the viewer, at a glance, to grasp the profound effects of time on a particular locale. As one enthusiastic trustee of the Society commented upon viewing the photographs, "It's about as close to a time machine as you can get." The comparisons can be startling, amusing, gratifying or, sometimes, even frustrating. The reactions we received as we shared our work with others along the way surprised even us. Viewers were stunned as they absorbed the photographic comparisons.

Duxbury has changed a great deal. Today, thanks to the foresight and dedication of the Town, numerous local organizations, and thousands of conscientious citizens, Duxbury is a community that is happily free of industrial and commercial sprawl. However, this was not always so. Shipyards, wharves, and mills once crowded Duxbury's shores. There was nothing pretty about them. Later, huge hotels and tumbledown shops sprang up at the end of the 19th century to cater to tourists. By the early 20th century, residents banded together to reverse these trends and, in a way, turned back the clock, removing the industrial sites, hotels and stores. These removals were not always planned, but nonetheless, Duxbury gradually began to return to something more unspoiled. Many might assume, for instance, that the idyllic marshes around the Bluefish River have always been that way. A glance at a few of these photographs will certainly alter their perceptions. While it is true that Duxbury has seen tremendous growth along residential lines, and certain areas such as Hall's Corner and Island Creek continue to expand commercially, the story of change in Duxbury, as evidenced by these photographs, is not so much a story of development as it is one of increased conservation and removal of the old industries.

Something must be said here about the most obvious element of change in Duxbury: trees. The dense forests that today surround us are often taken for granted. However, in studying these photographs, the first thing most viewers will notice is the astonishing lack of trees in 19th and early 20th century Duxbury. Historian Justin Winsor wrote in 1849 that the last of

Duxbury's isolated stands of primeval forest were cut down within the memory of many then living—probably around the 1820's. The need for firewood, building material and open agricultural fields stripped our community almost completely clear of foliage. Examining these photographs, it is no wonder that one of the first priorities of the Duxbury Rural Society, founded in 1883, was to plant hundreds of trees.

This phenomenon was not unique to Duxbury. By the mid 19th century, virtually all of New England had been deforested with the exception of northernmost Maine. Eventually, as agriculture declined in New England and other sources of lumber further west became available, new growth forests began to reclaim the landscape in the early 20th century. Trees are good for our environment and the many acres of conservation land now held by the Town and non-profit organizations enhance our quality of life, prevent development, and provide habitat for wildlife. A glance at these historical photographs of Duxbury, though, might serve to remind us that there is another natural resource that we seem to have lost sight of, in a way, and that is vistas. Who, for instance, can drive by the dramatic expanse of the

Bay Farm Conservation Area without turning their head to admire it? Vistas are all too few in Duxbury now, and those remaining should be preserved.

Aside from the changes, we were also struck by the way in which many elements of Duxbury have endured. While many of these views depict industrial and commercial sites that have simply vanished, others depict residential areas that are virtually unchanged. This is unusual for towns in Massachusetts and is indicative of a strong tradition of historic preservation in this town. Over the course of the 20th century, historic houses in all parts of Duxbury have endured and, we hope, will continue to do so for centuries to come.

It has been a fascinating project, walking in the footsteps of photographers of long ago. We hope our readers glean the same appreciation for Duxbury's remarkable change and endurance.

Patrick T.J. Browne
Norman R. Forgit
Duxbury Rural and Historical Society

Acknowledgments

First and foremost, we would like to thank local historian Tony Kelso who was most generous in enthusiastically sharing his extensive research and helping us to identify many buildings depicted in this publication.

We would also like to thank the Duxbury Rural and Historical Society's Publications Committee—William McArdle (Chairman), Katherine Pillsbury, Jayne Talmage, and Alice Vautrain—for their efforts in bringing the project to fruition. Kathy and Alice, as well as Tony Kelso, also provided assistance with editing. Thanks also to Bob Hale for providing information on 20th century Duxbury.

Jason Wolfson made the aerial photography possible by taking Norman and Jonathan Forgit up in his plane and circling the skies over Duxbury. Without his help, a key component of the book would not have been possible. Our thanks in this regard also go to Jonathan Forgit who shot several of the aerial photographs. Kerry Durkin, DRHS Archivist, helped locate some key photographs within the collections at the Society's Drew Archival Library.

While most of the photographs in *Duxbury…Past and Present* come from the Society's archives, images were also generously loaned by Rodney Brunsell, Raymond Day Jr. & Nell Day Hamilton, Tony Kelso, Brian Patenaude, Doris Prince, Rosamund Thompson, and the Massachusetts Historical Society through the assistance of Elaine Grublin.

A note about the images from the past

When researching early images for publication, the results can be exciting or, quite often, discouraging. We encountered a wide range of quality, the result of many factors. Much of the early photography was taken by amateur photographers, often with very primitive equipment. However, often an excellent original image becomes hard to work with because of age, mishandling, environmental conditions, etc. The end result sometimes is an image too good to ignore, but with poor reproductive quality. Also, some interesting images are small format snapshots which do not enlarge well. This is why some images in this book appear smaller or with less clarity than we would have hoped, but regardless, these are all images that we felt need to be saved for others to see.

Duxbury...

PAST & PRESENT

Patrick T. J. Browne
Norman R. Forgit

Nathaniel Porter Keene's Shipyard, Bluefish River, 1869

Views of Duxbury's famed shipyards are extremely rare as most went out of business before the age of photography. This is one of three such photographs. After the Civil War, a handful of enterprising young master carpenters felt they could rekindle the glory days of Duxbury shipbuilding. One of them was Nathaniel Porter Keene (1833-1920) who purchased the old Levi Sampson shipyard and began building vessels there around 1868. The vessel shown here is the Ship *Samuel G. Reed*, named after a Boston merchant. The economy of the post-Civil War era demanded large vessels—too large for Duxbury's shallow harbor. After constructing about five vessels, Keene launched his last, the *Henry J. Lippett*, in 1875. She was dubbed "Keene's Elephant" by cynical residents who knew that a Duxbury shipbuilding renaissance would not last long. When launched, the *Lippett* slammed into the opposite bank of the Bluefish River, leaving a 40 foot gouge in the marsh that some say is still visible today. Frustrated, Keene moved his operation to Weymouth.

***Bluefish River from
River Lane***

Today, there are few signs that thriving shipyards once existed along the Bluefish River. Wharves, sawpits, mills and warehouses have all been removed and the river's edge has now reverted to peaceful marsh. Many of the houses visible in the historical photograph are still present. Most noticeable is the yellow house at 10 Powder Point Avenue on the far right in both photographs, long known as the William Ellison House. The floodgates of the original, wooden Bluefish River Bridge are just visible immediately to the left of the ship in the historical photograph. Today's stone Bluefish River Bridge was constructed in 1883.

Partridge Academy,
Tremont Street,
_c. 1890_

George Partridge (1740-1828) led a distinguished political career, serving Duxbury and the Commonwealth of Massachusetts as a representative to the Provincial Court prior to the Revolution, then as a representative to the Continental Congress and the United States Congress. Upon his death, he left $10,000 for the establishment of a private secondary school in Duxbury. This led to the establishment of Partridge Academy (the building at right), completed in 1844. In 1868, an agreement was reached between the Academy trustees and the Town of Duxbury allowing all Duxbury students of secondary school age to attend, effectively making Partridge Academy Duxbury's first High School. The mustached man fourth from the left is Herbert Walker, long-time headmaster of the Academy. The building partially in view to the left is the Old Town Hall, constructed in 1840, and still in use as the Town Manager and Selectmen's Office.

Duxbury Town Offices, 878 Tremont Street

By the 1920's, the town had outgrown Partridge Academy. Plans were produced to construct a new high school building between Partridge Academy and the Old Town Hall, linking the two buildings. This plan was scrapped in favor of a new building off Alden Street, built in 1927. The School off Alden Street, now the home of the Duxbury Free Library, was Duxbury's first public high school. No longer needed, Partridge Academy sat vacant and eventually burned in 1933. The new Town Hall was constructed on the site of Partridge Academy in 1975.

5

Duxbury High School, off Alden Street, 1942

By 1926, Partridge Academy, a relatively small wooden building where the present Town Hall stands on Tremont Street, had served as the town's high school for more than 80 years. That ever-growing numbers of students were crammed into a structure built to suit 1840's Duxbury is almost unimaginable. Still, when the proposed new High School came up for a vote at the 1926 Town Meeting, it very narrowly passed the two-thirds vote required to move forward. After the vote passed, Selectman Alfred E. Greene rose and proposed that another vote be taken with all voting unanimously so that they could "all go home friends." The vote was called for and it was unanimous.

Duxbury Free Library, 77 Alden Street

When the new school was completed at a cost of $85,000, the High School Building Committee wrote in their 1927 report that "the building is a somewhat larger and better building in the opinion of the committee than was outlined to the Town. The building must speak for itself. The committee have done the best they could, and hope that the building will in future years be a great help and satisfaction to the Town." Indeed, the building has been a greater help to the Town than the committee could have imagined, first as the High School and now as the Duxbury Free Library. In 1997, the Library more than tripled its space by moving from the cramped Wright Building to airy, newly renovated quarters in the old Duxbury High School.

Captain George C. Prior House, c. 1900

George Prior, born in 1807, was part of a later generation of Duxbury sea captains who went to work for Boston merchants and ship-owners after most of the Duxbury merchant houses had failed around 1840. Prior was perhaps best known as master of the Bark *Smyrniote*, built in Duxbury in 1859 by William Paulding. The vessel was owned by a succession of Boston merchants and employed in the Mediterranean fruit trade. Prior's elegant house on Washington Street, built about 1851, is one of the few in town of Italianate design.

526 *Washington Street*   For much of the 20th century, the Prior House belonged to Winthrop Coffin, a mechanical engineer and executive of a turbine company. It is still often referred to as the "Coffin House." Although its ornamentation has been simplified, the house still retains is original Italianate elegance.

Alden House,
c. 1890

Long known as the John Alden House, the structure was once believed to be the second home of the famous Mayflower passengers John and Priscilla Alden. Recent research by James Baker, current Curator of the Alden House, and others, points towards a construction date of roughly 1672. This would indicate that the house was probably built by Jonathan Alden, son of John and Priscilla. Shortly before this photograph was taken, the house was divided into separate living spaces by two brothers, Capt. John ("Jack") Alden and Henry P. Alden. Capt. Jack, a retired mariner and Civil War veteran, inherited the eastern half. He was referred to by historian Dorothy Wentworth as a "jolly good fellow" who loved to talk and, after his children had moved out, lived alone in his half of the house with numerous cats. Henry, also a Civil War veteran, inherited the western half and lived there with his wife and four children.

Alden House Historic Site, 105 Alden Street

After the deaths of Capt. Jack and Henry P. Alden in 1887 and 1891 respectively, Capt. Jack's son, John W. Alden, eventually came to own both sides of the house. He was, however, forced to mortgage the house to John T. Alden, a distant relation from St. Louis, known to the Duxbury Aldens as a "rich cousin." John T. Alden had likely never seen the house before he bought it, but had grand visions of restoring the structure and making it a museum. Sadly, he lost his fortune and his health, and he was not able personally to bring his plans to fruition. It is fortunate, however, that his guardian had the good sense to sell the house in 1907 to the Alden Kindred of America, a new organization at the time. The Alden house, one of the oldest in Duxbury, has been operated as a museum for nearly 100 years.

Seth Sprague, Jr. House, c. 1910

Here we see what had been the elegant home of Seth Sprague, Jr. (1787-1856) and his wife, Welthea Little Sprague (1788-1892). Seth, Jr. was the son of Seth Sprague, Esq., one of Duxbury's most successful shipbuilders and regional leader of various social causes, including antislavery. Seth Sprague, Jr. followed in his father's footsteps, becoming a Massachusetts Senator and drafting legislation to counter Jim Crow laws. His house was built in 1813 on a portion of his father's vast estate. In this view, showing the Harrison Street side, Sweetser's Store can be seen in the background. In 1872, the house was purchased by a Mr. Hollis and converted into a hotel. The hotel went through a variety of owners and was known as the "Winsor Hotel" and the "Brunswick House." Judging by its appearance, this photograph was taken during a lull in the hotel's operation, probably just before it was purchased by Maurice Chandler.

476 *Washington Street*

When the house was purchased by Maurice Chandler (b. 1874) in 1912, it saw many invigorating changes. Before getting into the hotel business, Chandler had been a peddler in Plymouth. According to author Margery MacMillan, it was Chandler who had the Washington Street door cut and the orientation of the house was forever altered. Most passers-by would never suspect that the main door was originally on this Harrison Street side of the house. An attractive piazza (since removed) was built around the building and the hotel re-opened as the "Bayside Inn." It continued in operation until 1923. The building was converted to apartments in 1960 and then condominiums in 1981.

"Pine Hill" or
The Wright Estate,
c. 1930

The elegant estate shown here was built by the eldest son of Ezra Weston II "King Caesar." Gershom B. Weston constructed the mansion in 1857 to replace his earlier home on the site that had burned in 1850. Although not quite as influential as his father, Gershom was a powerful political presence in Civil War era Duxbury. Unfortunately, after the Weston firm closed in 1857, Gershom found himself deeply in debt to his brother Alden B. Weston. Alden, who had inherited the King Caesar House, eventually foreclosed on his brother, forcing Gershom and his family out of his mansion in 1869. Alden then sold the property to some intriguing newcomers to Duxbury—George and Georgianna Wright. In a way, the sale of the house represented the end of one era and the beginning of another—a transition from the Westons to the Wrights as Duxbury's most influential family. George Wright was an exceedingly wealthy cotton merchant raised in Brookline. Georgianna Wright was the daughter of a New York attorney.

**Eben Howes Ellison
High School,
130 St. George Street**

Georgianna Wright suffered many tragedies in her life, including the untimely deaths of two husbands and all four of her children. Perhaps the good that her family did for the Town of Duxbury brought her some satisfaction in the midst of her personal losses. The Wrights supported many fledgeling non-profit organizations in Duxbury, donated two buildings for the Duxbury Free Library, and assisted many local families in times of need. After Georgianna's death, Pine Hill was left to Harvard University, then acquired by the Ellison Family and, in 1966, given to the Town of Duxbury. By that time, the once-grand mansion was vacant and collapsing. It was torn down to make way for a new Middle School, now the High School. Today, all that remains of Pine Hill are the handsome stone gates to the school and the granite wall along St. George Street.

15

Gates of the Wright Estate,
St. George Street, c. 1915

The elegant gates and entry lane of the Wright Family estate, known as "Pine Hill," provide an excellent sense of the grandeur of the property. When George and Georgianna Wright purchased the property in 1869, they added a mansard roof and other Victorian ornamentation to the mansion (visible at left). They also built sunken gardens, showpiece barns for their prize-winning horses, and even a trotting track where today's Onion Hill Road presently runs.

Duxbury High School East Entrance, 130 St. George Street

When the Duxbury Middle School (now Duxbury High School) was constructed in 1968 on the site of the Wright mansion, vestiges of the gates to the old estate were retained at both entrances to the school. The wrought iron lanterns are long gone, but their imprints can still be seen in the granite. Hundreds of students pass through the gates each day, likely unaware of the fact that the curving granite walls were not built for the High School, but for George and Georgianna Wright nearly 100 years earlier.

Duxbury Free Library,
c. 1895

The Duxbury Free Library was first made possible in 1889 by a donation of $5,000 from Henry Winsor, a grandson of Duxbury shipbuilder Joshua Winsor. Winsor had moved to Philadelphia and ran a successful steamship company. The nascent library now had funds, but no home. This was provided in 1890 by George and Georgianna Wright who donated their guest house, opposite their opulent Pine Hill estate, for use as a library. The first Duxbury Free Library soon proved too cramped. Georgianna Wright had the building moved down the street where it still stands and funded a new brick building for the library in 1907.

The Wright Building,
147 St. George Street

Renovated by the Town of Duxbury and re-dedicated on September 22, 2007, the Wright Building now houses the Drew Archival Library of the Duxbury Rural and Historical Society and the Duxbury Student Union. The original, wooden Duxbury Free Library was located where the Reading Room, or eastern wing of the building now stands. During the recent renovation, part of an old granite foundation was uncovered and it is believed that a portion of the older library's foundation was incorporated in the Wright Building foundation.

178 St. George Street   The first Duxbury Free Library was moved to make way for the Wright Building in 1907 and now sits across the street from the Percy Walker Pool. After it ceased to be used for library purposes, it was taken over by various town departments and, for much of the 20th century, was known as the Town Offices. The building now houses private businesses.

Duxbury Free Library,
St. George Street, 1909

The building shown here was donated to the Town of Duxbury by Georgianna Wright (1837-1919) to replace the first, wooden Duxbury Free Library. Sparing no expense, she hired a well-known architect, Joseph Everett Chandler, to design a brick structure which was completed in 1909. A newspaper reporter present at the dedication noted some of the library's impressive features, including electric lighting and a reading room paneled in black cypress with gilded accents. The sign bracket evident in the photograph is still in use today.

The Wright Building,
147 St. George Street

The Duxbury Free Library moved to new quarters on Alden Street in 1997. Although used sporadically by various organizations for a few years, by 2004 the Wright Building was vacant and suffering decay. By a vote of Town Meeting, Community Preservation Funds were appropriated and the Town of Duxbury undertook the extensive restoration of the building in 2006. The 1909 portion of the library was outfitted for use by the Duxbury Rural and Historical Society for their Drew Archival Library where historic documents (including the majority of photographs in this publication) are preserved. The 1968 addition was refurbished for use by the Duxbury Student Union. The Wright Building was re-dedicated on September 22, 2007, just slightly over one hundred years after the corner stone was laid.

21

Long Bridge, c. 1915

George and Georgianna Wright, Duxbury's most generous philanthropists of the late 19th century, were involved in a variety of Duxbury civic affairs. They also purchased a great deal of real estate around town including most of Duxbury Beach. George Wright planned to carve the beach up into more than 250 cottage lots. To allow easy access to the development, he needed a bridge. Then known as "Long Bridge" or the "Gurnet Bridge," the first bridge to Duxbury Beach was constructed, mainly through George Wright's influence, in 1892. Wright succeeded in building a few cottages out on Duxbury Beach around 1885, however the Portland Storm of 1898 so devastated the beach that Wright abandoned his development plans.

Powder Point Bridge

In 1919 a non-profit corporation, the Duxbury Beach Association, purchased the beach, forever ensuring the preservation of an environmental treasure. In 1941, ownership of the bridge was transferred from Plymouth County to the Town of Duxbury. In the early morning of June 11, 1985, a fire broke out on the bridge causing serious damage. Subsequent inspections revealed more troubling structural problems unrelated to the fire. In 1986, the original oak and pine bridge was torn down. Several designs for replacements were brought to Town Meeting including bridges of concrete, steel and tropical hardwood. The hardwood design was selected and the new bridge opened on August 29, 1987. Although its often repeated claim-to-fame as "the longest wooden bridge in the world" is difficult to confirm, the Powder Point Bridge's importance to generations of residents and the historic character of Duxbury are undeniable.

23

Powder Point
School for Boys,
c. 1915

In 1886, Frederick B. Knapp (1857-1932) purchased the King Caesar House and the surrounding estate from the grandchildren of shipbuilder Ezra Weston II "King Caesar." Knapp, former Superintendant of Buildings at Harvard College, aimed to establish a preparatory school, converting King Caesar's barns into gymnasiums and classrooms. The school was known as the Powder Point School for Boys and quickly earned an excellent reputation. As shown here, Knapp added athletic fields, laboratories, and faculty housing. The building at right was the second student dormitory. In 1913 it replaced a smaller one built in 1893. In the summer, the dormitory doubled as a hotel. Left of center is the Grove House, now gone, which was primarily faculty housing. At far left is The Cottage, a combination of classrooms and employee housing, which still stands as 126 King Caesar Road.

South Shore of Powder Point

The Powder Point School for Boys operated successfully for nearly 40 years but eventually merged with Tabor Academy in the 1920's. The large dormitory was purchased by the National Sailors Home in 1931 and housed retired mariners for several decades. It was razed in 1975. With the exception of the field in the foreground, the campus is now heavily wooded. Houses on Moulton and Weston Roads now occupy the site of Frederick Knapp's athletic fields.

Washington Street was laid out in 1798, part of a controversial scheme of several shipbuilders (including Ezra Weston I "King Caesar"). Their goal was to create an avenue along the shore which would link the growing numbers of shipyards and wharves. Though the project was hugely controversial at first, it proved to be a boon to Duxbury's maritime economy. The street has alternately been known as "The Road to the Bluefish River," Main Street, and, finally, Washington Street. This view shows the intersection of Harrison and Washington Streets. The 1813 Seth Sprague, Jr. house is located on the left . The 1807 Nathaniel Winsor, Jr. House stands at right. Nathaniel Winsor, Jr. (1775-1859) inherited a sizeable fishing fleet from his father. His son, Nathaniel Winsor III (1806-c.1891) moved the family business to Boston and created the "Winsor Line," a fleet of clipperships that ran between Boston and San Francisco.

The Main Thoroughfare, Duxbury, Mass.

COPYRIGHT 1905, A. S. BURBANK, PLYMOUTH MASS.

SOLD BY N. M. STETSON, DUXBURY, MASS.

HELIOTYPE CO., BOSTON.

The Nathaniel Winsor, Jr. House,
479 Washington Street

Nathaniel Winsor's house remained in his family for three generations. It was purchased in 1902 by Thomas Kane and turned into a hotel known as "The Franklin House." In 1916, Maurice Chandler, who also owned and operated the adjacent Seth Sprague, Jr. House as a hotel, took over the Nathaniel Winsor, Jr. House and dubbed it the "Colonial Inn." In 1949, it was purchased by Dr. and Mrs. Edwin Leonard who ran a bed and breakfast in the house. It is presently the headquarters of the Duxbury Rural and Historical Society, having been purchased and restored after a community fundraising effort in 1997.

*Procession of
Civil War Veterans,
Mayflower Cemetery,
Memorial Day, 1913*

More than 200 men from Duxbury enlisted to serve in the Civil War, nearly 10% of the town's population at the time. The majority of them served in either the 18th or 38th Massachusetts Infantry Regiments. The 18th fought in Northern Virginia; the 38th in Louisiana. Duxbury's Civil War veterans continued to participate in Memorial Day ceremonies, as shown in this photograph, well into the 1920's. Duxbury's last surviving Civil War veteran, Albert Goulding, died in 1936.

Civil War Monument, Mayflower Cemetery, 774 Tremont Street

The Civil War monument in Mayflower Cemetery, where the veterans once fired salutes to their fallen friends, is still the site of annual Memorial Day ceremonies. Dedicated to the memory of "the soldiers and sailors who gave their lives for their country in the War of 1861," it bears the names of 37 men from Duxbury who were killed in the war.

**The Point School &
St. George Street, c. 1895**

In the 1870's, Duxbury's school districts were reorganized, prompting a wave of schoolhouse construction across town. Several of the one-room schoolhouses dating to this period still stand. The building just right of center in this view was the school for District #8, Powder Point. Known as the "Point School" (and later "Manion Hall"), it was constructed in 1878, replacing an older school of the same name that stood at the corner of Powder Point Avenue and Bay Pond Road on stilts over the marsh. The chimneys on the right belong to the 1829 Rebecca Frazar House at 56 St. George Street. Miss Frazar ran a respected private school there that continued well after her death.

**Ellison Center
for the Arts,
64 St. George Street**

The field in the foreground of the historic photograph was purchased by the Catholic Church in 1906. In 1934, Holy Family Church, Duxbury's first Catholic church, was constructed there. The Point School had ceased operation as an elementary school in 1927 and was purchased by the Church in 1954 to be used as a parish meeting hall. The building was re-named "Manion Hall" in honor of Holy Family's first pastor, the Rev. John Manion who served from 1945-1949. In 1988, the parish constructed a new larger Holy Family Church at the corner of Chestnut and Tremont Streets. The old church building on St. George Street was renovated and enlarged in 1997 and is now known as the Ellison Center for the Arts. It is home to the Duxbury campus of the South Shore Conservatory and the Duxbury Art Association. Manion Hall had to give way for the project. It was dismantled in 1996 and is now part of a house on Lincoln Street.

Cranberry Factory Mill,
_c. 1900_

This mill had nothing to do with cranberries. Its name defies explanation, but might have something to do with the proximity of several cranberry bogs. It was a textile mill and stood on the South River, just where it passes under Chandler Street. According to historian Dorothy Wentworth, it was "considered so picturesque in the 1890s that young ladies of that time painted it in oils or watercolors."

Cranberry Factory Pond, Chandler Street

The mill is long since gone. A visit to the site today, not far from the intersection of Chandler Street and Ledgewood Drive, will reveal only the earthen milldam and a trace of the old millrace. The millpond is still there, just a piece of it visible at right, and is known as Cranberry Factory Pond.

This is a view taken from near my grfather's house, showing the old store, and remains of Winsor's Wharf.

Winsor's Store & Wharves, by Justin Winsor, 1848

34

Shipbuilder and merchant Joshua Winsor (1749-1827) constructed Duxbury's first stone wharf in 1785. A second, adjacent wharf soon followed. His house, now gone, once stood close by. This was the heart of Winsor's thriving fishing enterprise. He was among the first of Duxbury's merchants to build schooners for the Grand Banks fishery and he profited greatly. By the time this view was sketched, Joshua was more than 20 years in the grave and his heirs were allowing the wharves to crumble. The scene was rendered by Joshua's great-grandnephew, Justin Winsor (1831-1897). A student at Harvard College at the time, Justin was in the midst of writing his *History of Duxbury*. He eventually went on to become head librarian of the Boston Public Library, one of the nation's leading historians, and a pioneer of early library science. The caption in upper right corner reads: *"This is a view taken from near my grfather's* [Nathaniel Winsor Jr.] *house, showing the old store and remains of Winsor's Wharf."*

Courtesy of the Massachusettts Historical Society

View from 32 Long Point Lane

Just north of the Duxbury Yacht Club, the rocky remains of Winsor's wharves can still be seen to this day at low tide. The pile of stones left of center in this photograph is all that is left of the northern wharf at which a schooner is tied in Winsor's sketch. After Joshua Winsor's death, Duxbury merchant George Frazar purchased his house and tore it down, building a new, Greek Revival building over the old Winsor foundation in 1831. The George Frazar House still stands today at 32 Long Point Lane, overlooking one of the few visible remnants of Duxbury's maritime era.

*Freeman's English
& West India Goods,*
c. 1900

Winfield Scott Freeman was Duxbury's most successful store keeper during the late 19th century. Born in 1839 and named for the nation's great military hero, General Winfield Scott, Freeman grew up in the vicinity of Hall's Corner. He pursued his father's trade, shoemaking, until around 1865 when he decided to break from family tradition and launched a career as a grocer and dry goods merchant. In setting up shop, Freeman purchased land along the east side of Washington Street from the Sprague family. There he had a one-room store and house where he resided until about 1877 when he built his elegant dwelling, still standing, at 37 Harrison Street. The one-room store grew and grew and eventually, around 1877, Freeman constructed a new building, very large for those days, that we now know as "Sweetser's." The original sign out front read, "W.S. Freeman & Co. English and West India Goods."

![Sweetser's Building photograph]

Sweetser's Building,
459 Washington Street

Around 1900, Freeman turned the business over to his step-son Fred Sweetser and his son-in-law Arthur Arnold. Both men had served as clerks for Freeman for many years. The store was thereafter known as "Sweetser & Arnold's" and, eventually, just "Sweetser's." At the turn of the century, it was one of the most booming businesses in town. There were departments for groceries, dry goods, shoes, house paint, rope and anchors, grain and baled hay, clothing, kitchen ware, furniture and countless other items. The building continued to serve as a general store until about 1990 when it was divided up for use as smaller offices and shops. It is, today, one of Duxbury's best known and most treasured landmarks, the heart of the Snug Harbor neighborhood.

37

Old Burying Ground, Chestnut Street, c. 1900

All but forgotten in the 19th century, Duxbury's first burying ground had become a dreadful tangle of brush and weeds by the 1880's. One of the first projects of the Rural Society, founded in 1883, was to clear the mysterious graveyard. The project was completed in 1887. In the course of doing so, curious researchers discovered what the community had long forgotten—that this was the resting place of Duxbury's first settlers and the site of the First Meeting House constructed around 1637. The photograph is an excellent example of the nearly treeless nature of Duxbury's landscape in the 19th century. Morton's Hole, the landing place frequently used by the first settlers, is clearly visible in the background at right. The combination of a protected cove, a nearby stream providing fresh water, and a high hill made the site ideal for the First Meeting House.

Standish Cemetery, Chestnut Street

Today, only a hint of Captain's Hill is visible in the background and the Myles Standish Monument at its peak is completely obscured. At right is the old stone locating the site of the First Meeting House (also visible in the historic photograph). It was joined in 1937 by a rectangular granite marker as part of Duxbury's effort to denote its historic places during the tercentennial celebration.

39

Myles Standish Gravesite, Old Burying Ground, Chestnut Street, 1893

When the long-neglected Old Burying Ground was reclaimed in 1887, many became fixated on the notion of finding the grave of Myles Standish, Duxbury's most popular historical figure at the time. Research indicated that the Standish plot was marked by two pyramid-shaped fieldstones. These stones were located and, after much debate, it was decided in 1889 to dig there in an attempt to find Standish's remains. The first dig proved inconclusive. Another was undertaken in 1891. This time, numerous skeletons were uncovered, all in one plot, and appeared to be consistent with the ages of various members of the Standish family at death. For this and other reasons, it was concluded that Myles Standish had been found. A suitably martial monument was placed over the gravesite in 1893, apparently just completed when this photograph was taken.

Myles Standish Gravesite, Chestnut Street

Myles Standish would be exhumed a third time. In 1930, descendants of Standish, evidently uneasy with the fact that the Captain had been reinterred in a pine coffin after the 1891 dig, desired to better preserve their ancestor's remains. And so a third dig was undertaken. Standish's remains were placed in a sealed copper box, and that box placed within a cement chamber under the monument. However, the descendants also added to the chamber a copper tube containing time capsule material. Thus, it appears that they expected Standish to someday be exhumed a fourth time. The monument over Standish's grave is meticulously cared for by the Town of Duxbury and the Standish Cemetery remains one of Duxbury's most tranquil and inspiring locations. Note the small sapling in the foreground of the historic picture appears to be the adult pine in the present day view.

Joseph Soule House,
c. 1890

An interesting example of a colonial house that was "Victorianized," the Joseph Soule House stands near the mouth of Eagle's Nest Creek. Soule, a yeoman, purchased most of Eagle's Nest Point and built a house there around 1774. Three generations of his family lived in the homestead. In 1871, it ended up in the hands of the Duxbury Shore Company. Owned by Boston businessmen, the company had purchased most of Standish Shore with an aim to create a paradise for summer visitors. One of the principal stockholders, James Cooke of Boston, purchased the Joseph Soule House and resided there with his family from about 1875 until 1881. It was probably Cooke who made the Victorian alterations. As it turned out, the Myles Standish Hotel they constructed was very popular, but the cottage lots did not sell well. Cooke sold the Soule house to Emma Drew in 1881. Drew, a widow, operated the property as a boarding house. This photograph was likely taken during the boarding house era.

152 Marshall Street

Exactly when the house was "de-Victorianized" and returned to something more like its original, colonial appearance is not known. Warren Sherburne of Lexington, superintendant of a construction company, used the house as a summer residence from 1907 until 1920. Harry Hunt, an engineer and public utilities executive, owned the property from 1920 to 1952. Either of these men might have restored the house to its present appearance. Today it stands as the oldest house on Marshall Street.

Duxbury Coal & Lumber Wharf, 1906

After most Duxbury shipyards closed in the 1840's and maritime commerce all but ceased, the once-busy stone wharves along Duxbury's shore began to fall into decay. That is, with one notable exception. William Sheldon, a lumber dealer, purchased a portion of what had been shipbuilder Seth Sprague's estate where Beaverbrook Lane now runs. He lived at 464 Washington Street, across from the Sweetser's Building, in one of the few Victorian houses in Snug Harbor. He also purchased Seth Sprague's wharf, repaired it and operated a successful business there known as the Duxbury Coal and Lumber Company. It was one of the few waterfront spots in late 19th century Duxbury that teemed with commercial activity, as shown in this photograph. The Nathaniel Winsor Jr. House, now the headquarters of the Duxbury Rural and Historical Society, is just visible at far left.

Duxbury Bay Maritime School, 457 Washington Street

The Duxbury Bay Maritime School was founded in 1997 with an aim towards connecting Duxbury's residents with the bay through sailing courses and other educational programs. By the time the DBMS came to occupy the property, Sprague's Wharf, later known as the Duxbury Coal and Lumber Wharf, had almost completely decayed. It was replaced in 2000 with a new bulkhead, boat launch and dock known as the South Boat Basin. This view will change significantly in the coming years as the DBMS implements a new building plan. Pilings for a new classroom building can be seen at center, oddly reminiscent of the schooner masts in the historic view. Perhaps the only recognizable feature is the white George Frazar House on Long Point Lane, hiding in the background toward the right of both photographs.

45

Morton's Hole, c. 1900

The shallow inlet to the west of the peninsula known as Captain's Nook has been known as Morton's Hole since the earliest days of Duxbury's settlement. It is one of Duxbury's most ancient place names. In fact, this modest little cove was of special significance to the first settlers of Duxbury. It was commonly used as a landing place and, given that the town's First Meeting House was constructed close by on today's Chestnut Street, Morton's Hole became something akin to the first "Duxbury Harbor." The cove was likely named after Thomas Morton, Jr. who owned a grant there in the 1630's. The Myles Standish Monument, towering above the scene before trees reclaimed Captain's Hill, was completed in 1898.

Morton's Hole viewed from Bay Road

The inlet is essentially as peaceful now as it was a century ago. Tall phragmites grasses are slowly taking over the scene, and enormous white pines have obscured all but the top of the Myles Standish monument. But the view retains much of the same character as its older counterpart.

47

The Town House, 1910

Both the First Parish Church and the Town of Duxbury constructed new buildings in 1840 along Tremont Street. They were constructed in the new Greek Revival Style which, at the time, was bold, striking and meant to inspire respect. The Town House, seen here at center, was used not only for town business, but also for a variety of lectures. Just visible through the trees to the right is Partridge Academy, also in the Greek Revival Style, which joined the two buildings in 1844 to form a formidable triumvirate of church, government, and education.

The Old Town Hall,
878 Tremont Street

The 1840 structure is still used by the Town, although in examining the interior, it is difficult to imagine the small space had ever been used as a meeting hall. It presently houses the Town Manager and Selectmen's Office. The woods on either side of Depot Street are known as Lapham Woods and were purchased by the Duxbury Rural Society in 1931. The Society had had their eyes on the property for more than 15 years, feeling it was vital that the land be protected to prevent the arrival of gas stations, garages and various shops at the intersection that would distract from the impact of the elegant trio of Greek Revival buildings.

49

THE MYLES STANDISH
SOUTH DUXBURY, MASS.

(OVER)

Myles Standish Hotel,
c. 1900

In 1871, a group of Boston entrepreneurs formed the Duxbury Shore Company and built a hotel known as the Standish House, later known as the Myles Standish Hotel, which eventually grew to become the complex shown here. They also laid out plans for a huge development of summer cottages along a new road constructed in 1872 called Columbus Avenue (now Marshall Street). Although very few cottages were actually built, the hotel was tremendously popular. It was, author Margery MacMillan noted, not just a retreat for well-to-do Bostonians and New Yorkers, but also the center of social life for locals as well. The hotel featured richly appointed rooms, tennis courts, a 9 hole golf course, daily concerts, weekly balls, a natural spring and a 400 foot, illuminated pier from which regattas were launched.

Standish Shore   A fire broke out in the garages behind the hotel in 1908. Although damage to the hotel itself was relatively minor, tough economic times caused it to close in 1910. The huge building sat boarded-up until 1914. Finally, new owners decided to raze the center of the hotel and to convert the now separated north and south wings into private homes. The north wing of the hotel (the right side of the building in the historical drawing) still sits in its original location, now 262 Marshall Street. It is the white house near the center of this photograph. The south wing (the left side) was moved a bit south to become 286 Marshall Street. It shows in the modern photograph as the building at far left with the enclosed veranda.

51

View of Millbrook, c. 1890

The area shown here, where Tremont Street crosses the Duck Hill River, has played a vital role in the history of Duxbury since the town's earliest days. In 1639, this was chosen as the site of Duxbury's first grist mill, owned by William Hiller. As colonists needed a mill to grind their grain for flour, a gristmill was key to any settlement's survival. The construction of the old Pilgrim-era mill gave the area its name—Millbrook—which is still in use today. By the time this photo was taken the grist mill was long gone and the site dominated by the old Weston Mill built by Ezra Weston I "King Caesar" in 1812 to produce sailcloth. The house in front of the mill is known as the Crab Island House and still stands today. The lack of trees allowed a view clear to Marshfield.

View from Cow Tent Hill, off Tremont Street

Clearly, there is no lack of trees today. The hill from which these photographs were taken is known as Cow Tent Hill—one of the more unusual Duxbury place names. According to tradition, hollows in the hill were covered with sailcloth to shelter cows in the 19th century. Like much of Duxbury, the hill has been reclaimed by trees. It is now conservation land owned by the Wildlands Trust.

53

Powder Point from Snug Harbor, c. 1895

In this rare, early view of Duxbury's waterfront, we see how the natural shoreline once appeared before the area was transformed into today's Town Landing and Town Dock. In the distance, the King Caesar House is visible at left amidst a largely treeless Powder Point. At left, in the foreground, the remains of Winsor's Wharves are quite distinct. Now only rubble marks the place where they once stood.

Snug Harbor   The gently sloping shoreline has since been replaced by the cement bulkheads surrounding the Town Dock and the Duxbury Bay Maritime School. The King Caesar House is still visible in the distance at left. The single dinghy visible in the historic photograph is now replaced by scores of pleasure craft moored in Duxbury Harbor.

55

Duxbury Village,
c. 1913

While Hall's Corner is now considered Duxbury's primary business district, at the turn of the century the main commercial area was at "the other flagpole" at the intersection of St. George and Washington Streets. This view depicts the area then known as "Duxbury Village" along Washington Street just north of the Bluefish River Bridge. The district had livery stables, a garage, a grocery store, a restaurant, a barber shop and a bowling alley among other establishments.

Washington Street north of the Bluefish River Bridge

In 1916, Clara Smith Ripley, a Drew descendant, purchased the Drew House, then known as the Union Store, and donated it to the Duxbury Rural Society for use as their "historical rooms." With a foothold in Duxbury Village, it became a priority of the Rural Society to "clean up" the area. Bit by bit, the Society acquired most of property on either side of Washington Street north of the Bluefish River Bridge and the ramshackle stores were removed. This effort was begun shortly after the Pilgrim Society's successful undertaking to clear Cole's Hill in Plymouth of its dilapidated commercial buildings. The Duxbury "Rurals" were likely inspired by their Plymouth counterparts.

57

**Hall's Corner
from Standish Street,
c. 1955**

Most of buildings on the block shown here were constructed about 1919. At that time, the commercial center of Duxbury was gradually shifting from one end of Washington Street to the other. Once-sleepy Hall's Corner would thereafter become Duxbury's main business area. The building on the right was Munro's Pharmacy, a popular hang-out due to the soda fountain there. Next was the old A&P Grocery Store. Next to the left was Toabe's Hardware Store. The last visible building on the block was the Duxbury 5 & 10. The flags at left mark the location of Cushing's auto dealership lots, at the corner of Washington Street and Depot Street, once the site of Hall's Tavern, for which the corner was named.

Hall's Corner
from Standish Street

The exterior of this block has remained virtually the same with no major alterations to the buildings. Although, today one would find very different establishments inside.

First Parish Church,
c. 1900

The Greek Revival First Parish Church was constructed in 1840, replacing the Third Meeting House, a structure in the Georgian architectural style that had stood on the site since 1786. By the 1830's, many of the congregation's families had grown wealthy through shipbuilding and maritime trade. They desired a more impressive church in the latest architectural style that would reflect Duxbury's prosperity. When built, the new church boasted the largest assembly hall in the region. The window set in the front pediment was designed to depict a globe, representing Duxbury's strong ties to international commerce. In this photograph, the two bicyclists are Ruby H. Graves and Paul Peterson.

First Parish Church, 842 Tremont Street

The church, now a Unitarian-Universalist congregation, is splendidly preserved and has changed very little since the 19th century. The Old Town Hall is visible at right.

Duxbury Post Office, c. 1904

The exact age of this building is not known. It was originally an outbuilding in one of the shipyards along the Bluefish River and probably dates to roughly 1820. In 1850, it was purchased by Zenas Faunce, who ran a blacksmith shop and other establishments in the area. He moved it to its present location at the corner of Washington Street and Fort Hill Lane and outfitted it as a post office in which capacity it served for about 60 years. According to researcher Virginia Seaver, the appellation "Bos'ns Locker" which is presently inscribed on a sign outside the building, was derived from the fact that, even when it was a post office, its loft was still stocked with cordage and other supplies related to the shipyards. Its loft was also, in the late 19th century, used as a small shoe factory.

One Fort Hill Lane

Around 1909, a new post office was constructed next door and the Faunce heirs converted the Bos'ns Locker into a gift shop. It operated as such until 1943 when it was sold off as a private residence, which it has been ever since. Clearly visible in the background of the historic photograph but difficult to discern in the present day view is the 1804 Daniel Peterson House at 6 Fort Hill Lane. It served as a boarding house for shipyard workers in the early 19th century and was later known as the Duxbury Inn.

*Ford's Store,
Tremont Street,
c. 1910*

One of Duxbury's best-known landmarks in the 19th century, Ford's Store was established in 1826 and originally known as "James T. Ford and Co." The Ford brothers were energetic and creative in their approach to business. Not satisfied to simply run a general store, they added all manner of rare imported items to their inventory. As historian Katherine Pillsbury observed, they were so successful that, in order to expand, they had to seek out old buildings to add on to the original store including a barn and an old blacksmith shop. Soon the store, a haphazard cluster of structures, stretched over 100 feet along Tremont Street.

1296 Tremont Street   The establishment often referred to as "America's Oldest Department Store" burned in 1921. The site today, aside from a stone marker on Tremont Street, bears virtually no indication that the busy operation ever existed. The store's neighbor at 1296 Tremont Street, known as the Old Ordinary (once a tavern), was probably built in the 17th century, and is visible at far right in both views.

Myles Standish Monument, c. 1895

Shortly after the Civil War, the town of Duxbury, suffering an economic slump due to the loss of the shipbuilding industry, found hope in the form of tourists. Many Bostonians sought out Duxbury's tranquil shores. They marveled at the town's natural beauty and its remarkable history. Visitors were particularly fascinated with Myles Standish, the Captain of the Pilgrims, popularized in Longfellow's The Courtship of Myles Standish. To celebrate Standish's fame (and to attract even more visitors) the Standish Monument Association was formed to construct what would be the nation's second tallest monument to an individual (surpassed only by the Washington Monument). 10,000 people attended the laying of the cornerstone in 1872. Unfortunately, the Association could not raise enough funds to finish the monument. Their efforts were severely hampered by the Panic of 1873, and construction halted for many years. This photograph appears to have been taken just after the resumption of construction.

Myles Standish Monument, off Crescent Street

When construction resumed, a slightly different color granite was used. The division between the two is clearly visible in the present day photograph. The monument was completed in 1898. 116 feet overall, at the peak stands a 14 foot statute of Standish holding out the scrolled charter of Plymouth Colony towards England. Numerous photographs taken from the top of Captain's Hill in the early 20th century depict a striking panorama. Historian Justin Winsor wrote in 1849 that an individual standing on Captain's Hill could look east to Provincetown and northwest to the Blue Hills. Due to the growth of white pines, this breathtaking view is now only available those who are willing to climb the 126 steps to the top of the monument.

67

Grand Army of the Republic Hall, Massachusetts Post #165 1904

The Grand Army of the Republic was a fraternal organization of veterans of the Union army who served in the Civil War. The Duxbury G.A.R. Hall, formed in 1885, was named for Pvt. William Wadsworth, a Duxbury mariner. He died on July 24, 1863 of wounds received in the assault on Port Hudson, Louisiana after languishing in a Baton Rouge hospital for nearly a month. The Hall had originally been a barn, constructed around 1850. Duxbury's Civil War Veterans continued to participate in civic events well into the 1920's.

569 Washington Street

As the veterans aged, the Hall was turned over to an affiliate organization, the Sons of Union Veterans of the Civil War. Duxbury's branch of the SUVCW was organized in 1895 and had an active membership, meeting at the Hall until 1955. The last surviving Duxbury veteran, Albert Goulding, died in 1936. When the nation's last Union Civil War veteran died in 1956 at age 109, the G.A.R. as a whole was officially dissolved. The Duxbury Sons of Veterans decided to donate the Hall, library, and many Civil War artifacts to the Duxbury Rural and Historical Society. The Society chose not to retain the Hall, but kept many of the Civil War artifacts which are frequently displayed. The Hall itself has been a private residence ever since.

Freeman's Variety Store, Hall's Corner, c. 1950

This deceptively old structure, originally a slaughterhouse on Harden Hill, was built around 1850 according to historian Tony Kelso. It belonged to the Westons and meat was probably prepared here to provision their ships. In 1874, it was purchased and moved by James and Caroline Myrick and attached to their new house and shop (now One Bay Road). Myrick used it as part of his tinsmith shop. It was later detached. In 1932, it was leased to Walter "Ducky" Freeman and his wife. The Freemans lived in an elaborate cottage at 68 Depot Street (see photo bottom right). Their yard featured a large, cement replica of the Statue of Liberty, the pedestal of which is still extant. Their store offered the only public pay phone at Hall's Corner and, because it was about the only place in town where records were sold, it was very popular with teenagers.

8 Standish Street   Freeman's Variety Store moved across the street in 1956. Since then the building has served as a variety of establishments including a dentist's office, interior decorating shop, and now a hair salon. Its larger neighbor in the background, One Bay Road, has shifted in position. The building first faced Standish Street, has been moved at least twice, and now faces in towards the Hall's Corner flagpole.

Nathaniel Winsor, Sr. House, c. 1900

Beginning in the 1780's, Nathaniel Winsor, Sr. (1747-1839) and his brother Joshua (1749-1827) teamed up to build one of Duxbury's earliest and most successful fishing fleets. By 1800, the Winsors had become quite prosperous and Nathaniel could afford to build a new and stylish house on Washington Street. The house remained in his family for 90 years. In 1905 the house was sold to Nellie A. Clapp of Duxbury whose husband, William F. Clapp, was a professor at MIT and former Curator of Mollusks at Harvard University. A Federal Committee, organized in response to the catastrophic failure of numerous wharves in San Francisco, tapped Clapp to conduct studies on the deterioration of marine building materials. In 1933, Professor Clapp converted Winsor's old barn into a laboratory.

405 Washington Street, Battelle Institute

The William F. Clapp Laboratories, Inc. became renowned for their studies in marine science. When Clapp died in 1951, the presidency of the organization passed to marine biologist Albert F. Richards and the operation continued to grow. In 1965, shortly after Richards's death, the laboratories became part of the Battelle Memorial Institute, based in Columbus, Ohio. Today, Battelle's Duxbury location continues to thrive.

William Martin Brewster House, c. 1880

According to research by local historian Robert Dente, William Martin Brewster, a rigger by trade, built the house shown here on the south shore of Powder Point in 1824. Brewster was a relative (first cousin once removed) of merchant Ezra Weston II, "King Caesar." The small piece of land on which Brewster built his house was purchased from his wealthy cousin. It is likely that Brewster worked for King Caesar, helping to rig some of Duxbury's most famous vessels. In 1856, Alden Cushman, a laborer born in Duxbury in 1822, purchased the house and lived there until his death around 1905. The man and woman featured in this photograph are probably Alden Cushman and his wife Jane along with their two children, Helen and Willie.

151 King Caesar Road   Aside from a few windows added to take advantage of a striking view across Duxbury Bay, the original portion of the house today stands much the same as William Martin Brewster built it.

HALLS CORNER, SO. DUXBURY MASS. 6.

**Hall's Tavern &
the Nook School,
October 17, 1913**

One of the earliest extant photographs of Hall's corner, this remarkable view shows, left to right, Hall's Tavern (for which the Corner was named), the Nook School (in the background), H.G. Freeman's shop, and the Harvey Soule House (far right) which once stood on the corner of Standish and Washington Streets. Hall's Tavern, built c. 1810, belonged to Capt. Daniel Hall and was, for the better part of a century, the only substantial building at what was then a very quiet corner. The Nook School was built in 1874 as part of a wave of one-room schoolhouse construction across Duxbury in that decade. The Harvey Soule House, finally offering a counterpoint to lonely Hall's Tavern, was built c. 1870.

Hall's Corner   In 1930, Hall's Tavern was dismantled and moved to Cambridge (20 Gray Gardens West) where it still sits today. Its site was occupied during the mid 20th century by show lots for the Cushing auto dealership and now the Exxon Station shown here. The Nook School still stands, though obscured by trees in this view, and is more commonly known as the Girl Scout House or the Duxbury Recreation Department. H.G. Freeman's shop was built c. 1875, moved by 1915 and may now be part of the Dole & Dowd store at 18 Washington Street. Beginning in the 1910s, Hall's Corner began to transition from a quiet crossroads to the busy commercial area we know today. The Harvey Soule House was moved in 1917 when the block of stores shown at right was planned. It is now 11 Washington Street.

Cox's Corner, c. 1950

Known as Five Corners in the early 19th century, this important crossroads near the Marshfield line is the junction of Church, Enterprise, and Tremont Streets. This portion of Tremont Street was once known to early settlers as the Green Harbor Path, and it was at this crossroads that the old colonial path bent east towards Green Harbor. In 1850, Charles Cox, a shoemaker, was the first to build a house at this corner (now 4 Duck Hill Road) and the intersection would thereafter bear his name. The establishment shown here was built in the mid 20th century and was once known as Dutchland Farms, where ice cream and sandwiches were sold. Later it was a popular candy shop.

**1508 Tremont Street,
Cox's Corner**

In the late 1960's, a fire destroyed the store and the lot sat vacant for more than 20 years. In 1990, the present retail and office buildings were constructed.

Eagles Nest from Harden Hill Road,
c. 1910

Justin Winsor tells us in his 1849 *History of Duxbury* that Eagles Nest Point (in the distance) was one of the last places in Duxbury to hold a stand of primeval forest. The place was named by the Pilgrim settlers and even into Winsor's era, eagles commonly nested in the ancient trees. That is, Winsor writes, "until of late years," because the last of the trees had been cut down. The area in the foreground was, in the early 19th century, the site of a shipyard known as the "Navy Yard" because of the large size of vessels launched there. In the 1810's it was owned by shipwright Benjamin Prior. From 1822 to 1834, it belonged to Ezra Weston II "King Caesar" and many of his famous vessels were built here. It is possible that the small building at center was an old outbuilding dating back to the shipyard days.

![Photograph of a tranquil shoreline with boats on the water, marshland, and a rocky beach in the foreground]

***End of
Harden Hill Road***

Trees have reclaimed Eagles Nest Point, though the eagles are not likely to return to nest there. King Caesar abandoned the Navy Yard in favor of an even larger shipyard he built on the south bank of the Bluefish River in 1834 called the "Ten Acre Shipyard." Ever since shipbuilding ceased, the area in the foreground has been a tranquil town landing. Today, there is no evidence of the busy shipbuilding that once took place there.

old House May 1919

Thomas Delano House, High Street, May 1919

The building shown here was constructed around 1667 by a son of Philip Delano, one of the first settlers of Duxbury. Philip Delano's farm was on the north side of what is now St. George Street. His neighbor on the south side of the lane was John Alden. It is therefore not surprising that one of Philip's sons married one of John's daughters. What is surprising is that Thomas and Rebecca chose to settle far from the farms along the shore, instead building on the "Bay Path" that ran from Plymouth to Boston. Although the road was well traveled, the house was quite isolated. Delanos occupied the property for almost 200 years. By 1919, when the photograph at left was taken, the house was falling into sad neglect.

Thomas Delano House, High Street, c. 1930

By the 1930's, some attempts at improvements had been made, including the unusual dormer, but the house still awaited a new lease on life.

82

261 High Street In 1933, the house was bought by Gleason Archer, Dean of Suffolk Law School, who in conjunction with Miss Carrolla Bryant restored the old homestead. It was, researcher George Gardener tells us, suffering from terrible decay. That they saved the structure is remarkable and fortunate for the community. It stands among the very oldest houses in town and is an important part of Duxbury's heritage.

*Duxbury Hall &
the Corner Stone
Masonic Lodge,
Washington Street, 1908*

In 1873, a group of civic-minded Duxbury women formed The Unitarian Aid Society to raise funds for charitable purposes. The group purchased in 1876 the building shown at right for their activities hall. Once located southeast of the Bluefish River Bridge, it had originally been a timber storage loft for the shipyard of Levi Sampson in the 1820s. Around 1865 it was moved to its present location by Peleg Brooks who used it as a livery stable. The Unitarian Aid Society raised money there by renting the hall out for lectures, dances, plays, dinners, concerts and balls. There was also a reading room and lending library. Given the year it opened, it was originally dubbed Centennial Hall. But, somehow, the name "Duxbury Hall" stuck. The building partially in view to the left is the original Duxbury Corner Stone Lodge.

Duxbury
Corner Stone Lodge
A.F. & A.M.,
585 Washington Street

The Duxbury Corner Stone Lodge was chartered in 1801. The members met at a variety of locations until 1825 when their first Temple (at left in the historic photograph) was constructed. The building served them well for more than a century but by the mid 20th century, they sought to expand. In 1958, their neighbors, the Unitarian Aid Society, gave up Duxbury Hall in favor of the new Elder Brewster Parish Hall which had been added on to the First Parish Church. After the Masons acquired Duxbury Hall, they moved their original building, attaching it to the front of Duxbury Hall. The combined structure, its origins rooted in Duxbury's shipbuilding era, continues to serve as the Corner Stone Lodge A.F. & A.M.

85

Winslow's Blacksmith Shop, c. 1933

Known at various times as J.K. Kemple's Wagon Shop and H.S. Winslow's Blacksmith Shop, the building in the foreground stands in Pembroke. By the time this photograph was taken, it had begun providing wagons of a different sort with gasoline. The High Street Methodist Church, in the background, is located in Duxbury.

High Street Methodist Church, 298 High Street

The first building owned by a Methodist congregation in Duxbury is now the Church of St. John the Evangelist and was built in 1823. Another Methodist Church was built on High Street in 1868. The area at the time was a growing village with its own post office and busy stores. Today, the stores such as Winslow's Blacksmith Shop are a thing of the past and High Street is a quiet residential area.

*Dr. Nathaniel Noyes
House,
Washington Street,
c. 1895*

Researcher Robert Dente tells us that Nathaniel K. Noyes (1865-1945) graduated from Dartmouth Medical School in 1889, married, and moved to Duxbury in 1892. He built his handsome house in 1894, a relatively rare example of Victorian architecture in town. His occupation as a village doctor required Noyes to travel across town for house calls, often at late hours and in dreadful weather. In the carriage house at right, he kept a sleigh for such calls in the winter. The street lamp in this photograph is believed to be one of the those set out by the Rural Society in the 1880's as their first village improvement project (hence the lamp is the logo of the Duxbury Rural and Historical Society today).

561 and 555 Washington Street   Dr. Noyes's carriage house has since been converted into a residence and still retains much of its original architecture. Although the verandah has been removed, the house itself remains virtually the same.

Pilgrim By-Way,
late 19th century

The cart path shown here, now known as Pilgrim By-Way, does not show up on Duxbury maps until 1913, although it was probably in existence well before that. When the railroad came through in 1871, a station was established at the corner of South Station and Depot Streets and Pilgrim By-Way suddenly became a convenient short-cut to the depot for those traveling along Chestnut Street. Although the date of this photograph is difficult to determine, it may have been taken in the 1880's before the Rural Society set about clearing the Old Burying Ground to the right of Pilgrim By-Way.

Pilgrim By-Way   The historic photograph is simply identified as "Pilgrim By-Way" and, given the utter lack of landmarks, it is difficult to determine exactly what part of the lane is pictured. The view above shows the road as seen today from Chestnut Street. Although it may not be precisely the same vantage point as the historic photograph, the present day view does provide a sense of the striking changes the little lane has seen over the 20th century.

91

Dunster Place, Standish Street, c. 1910

Shown during a period of neglect, this house is believed to have been moved from Kingston around the 1770's and was once occupied by a Revolutionary War soldier, Ezra Howard, who died on a prison ship. During the latter part of the 19th century, it was occupied by Henry J. Dunster, a laborer of modest means who happened to be a descendant and namesake of the first president of Harvard College. The house was long known as the "Dunster Place."

279 Standish Street Now attractively restored, the house's historical significance to its neighborhood is enhanced by the fact that it came so dangerously close to abandonment and demolition.

94 *Snug Harbor, 1946*

This aerial view was taken for the William F. Clapp Laboratories (now owned by the Battelle Institute) which occupied the complex of buildings at center. In the lower left corner is Sprague Hall. The building was originally part of Seth Sprague's shipyard which occupied that site in the early 19th century. Sprague converted the building into a meeting hall for Duxbury's first Methodist congregation in 1821, making it one of Duxbury's first community centers. Sprague Hall was later used by the Order of Odd Fellows, the League of Women Voters and by the Church of St. John the Evangelist as a parish house.

Snug Harbor   The large marsh flats in the historic photograph are presently occupied by Bayside Marine. Battelle Institute continues
to grow, having added numerous laboratories since the 1946 photograph was taken. Sprague Hall is still standing and
visible at the bottom center of the photograph. It was moved back from Washington Street and converted to a residence
at 9 Beaverbrook Lane. Perhaps most striking are the enduring remains of the two wharves, just as prominent today as they
were in 1946. The wharf to the right was known as Sampson's Wharf. Both date to roughly 1810 and linger as ghostly
reminders of Duxbury's shipbuilding era.

The building in the background was built in 1874 and served as the elementary school for Duxbury's 2nd school district—the Nook and Hall's Corner. With the eventual construction of new schools, most of Duxbury's one room schoolhouses fell out of use in the 1920's and 30's and were turned over to other community uses.

28 Washington Street   The Girl Scout House, as it came to be known in the 20th century, houses the offices Duxbury Recreation Department and is still used for community events.

Josephus Dawes House,
c. 1865 and 1879

Probably Duxbury's finest example of Second Empire architecture, the building's exact date of construction is unknown. We do know that its original configuration—a basic Cape Cod House as shown at left c. 1865 — was far more humble. In 1857, Captain Josephus Dawes purchased the house. Living so close to the Kingston line, Dawes apparently felt a pull in that direction. With most Duxbury merchant houses folding by the 1840s, Dawes chose to work for Kingston's most prominent merchant, Joseph Holmes. He captained numerous large vessels for Holmes and made a name and a considerable fortune for himself in the Mediterranean fruit trade in the 1860's. Dawes remodeled his simple Cape around 1872. A curiosity in a town that was, by and large, experiencing a depression, the house was featured in this sketch for the *1879 Plymouth County Atlas*, shown below.

RESIDENCE OF CAPT. JOSEPHUS DAWES, DUXBURY, MASS.

158 Tremont Street   The same view shown in the 1879 atlas is today obstructed by trees, and so we show the elegant Captain Dawes House here from a different angle. The house, outbuildings and even the fence out front remain the same.

Powder Point School Campus & King Caesar Road, 1896

This sketch was drawn for a promotional pamphlet for Powder Point Hall (at right) which, in addition to serving as the dormitory for the Powder Point School for Boys, doubled as a hotel in the summer. The headmaster of the school, Frederick B. Knapp, held considerable real estate on Powder Point and therefore the pamphlet also represented an effort to attract summer people who might build cottages on the Point. The pleasant view shows (from left to right) what had been King Caesar's Wharf, the King Caesar House (then the headmaster's house), the Cottage (classrooms and faculty housing), and Powder Point Hall, built in 1893 and replaced in 1913 after it burned.

King Caesar Road

King Caesar Road today follows the same bend. Remarkably, King Caesar's Wharf, built c. 1790, is still present, the only survivor of Duxbury's many maritime era stone wharves. It was gifted to the Duxbury Rural and Historical Society in 1945 by Hermon C. Bumpus, Jr. and is today known as Bumpus Park. The King Caesar House still stands, of course, but is not visible in this view. The Cottage is still present as well at 126 King Caesar Road and visible here. Several residences now occupy the lot where the dormitory once stood.

101

Hall's Corner, c. 1965   The establishment at the left end of the block in the background was Barnes's "Self Service" Market and Liquor Store, a long-time landmark at Hall's Corner. The next building to the right is the old Duxbury 5 & 10. At far right, in the foreground, can be seen the brick Freeman Building, built c. 1934, now the "anchor" of Hall's Corner. It originally contained a market, a furniture store, a Chevrolet dealership and a Mobil gas station.

Hall's Corner from Chestnut Street

The building that housed Barnes's Market has been modified a bit and a verandah added to the Freeman Building. Nevertheless, virtually all the buildings constructed at Hall's Corner during its dramatic commercial transformation in the 1920's and 30's are still there.

The King Caesar House,
c. 1932

Completed in 1809, the house built for Ezra Weston II "King Caesar" stands today as one of Duxbury's most historic buildings. From here, Weston managed the largest shipbuilding and mercantile operation on the South Shore. In 1886, Frederick B. Knapp converted the estate into the Powder Point School for Boys and the house became his residence as headmaster. Frederick and his wife Fanny Knapp died in 1932 and 1934, respectively. The house declined rapidly after their deaths. This photograph was likely taken about that time, given the house's appearance. In 1937 it was purchased by Dr. Hermon Bumpus, former director of the Museum of Natural History in New York, who thoroughly restored the mansion.

The King Caesar House Museum, 120 King Caesar Road

As revealed by the present day view, Bumpus removed portions of the house. The extended ell off the back was taken down. Beneath the ell, Bumpus found the remains of King Caesar's old ice cellar. This discovery reinvigorated old myths of a "smuggling cellar" and even a secret tunnel beneath the house. Simply legend, these myths persist today. Bumpus had the cellar filled in and the driveway behind the house currently runs over it. Just visible at the left of the historical photograph is the Victorian verandah added to the west side of the house by the Knapps. Bumpus removed this as well, restoring that façade to its original appearance. In 1965 the house was acquired by the Duxbury Rural and Historical Society and, on June 25, 1967 was dedicated as a museum, "commemorative of the busy shipbuilding days of Duxbury."

Myron M. White House,
c. 1910

White, who built this stylish house in 1904, was South Duxbury's postmaster at the time. We can only assume that he built his house here so as to be conveniently close to the post office at Hall's Corner which, in the early 20th century, changed locations numerous times. It was located in the Harvey Soule House for some time which stood where Duxbury Liquors is now, and also in a general store that once operated out of 11 Standish Street.

38 Standish Street   The house has lost its verandah and balcony, but otherwise has changed little from the time of its construction. The carriage house appears to be utterly unchanged.

107

Cushing Brothers Garage,
Hall's Corner, 1913

Parade Float in front of
the Cushing Brothers Building,
July 4, 1971

For the foresighted Cushing Brothers, it must have been a dramatic change going from horseshoes to auto parts. They were, however, quite successful. By the 1920's they had constructed their second and far more substantial garage and dealership shown at right. The business remained in the family for most of the 20th century. It was, at various times, a Hupmobile and later a Dodge dealership. Their show lots were across the street on the vacant lot where Hall's Tavern had once stood and where the Exxon Station stands now.

5 Chestnut Street

The Cushing Brothers Building, although significantly modified, still stands at the corner of Chestnut and Depot Streets. Today, the building is best known for the Dunkin Donuts it houses.

In 1870, Levi H. Cushing (1829-1913) purchased the 1818 Charles Soule House which once stood where Duxbury Pizza is now at 7 Standish Street (the house, now 1 Harden Hill Road, was moved back to make way for the commercial buildings around 1919). Cushing started up one of Duxbury's most successful livery stables. The business prospered by running guests from the depot at South Station Street to the Myles Standish Hotel. By the time he died, Cushing owned most of the land around Hall's Corner. Two of his sons, Earle and Paul, helped with the family business, shoeing horses and repairing buggies. By 1905, automobiles began to appear in Duxbury and it was clear that the days of the livery stable were limited. By 1913, the Cushing brothers had built the garage shown above, probably located on their father's property on Standish Street.

Eben and Grace Ellison House, Powder Point, c. 1905

Prior to the construction of Eben and Grace Ellison's summer house (at left), the entire area, according to researcher Karen Davis, was slated for a 250 lot development of small summer cottages to be known as Bay View Park. Lanes were actually laid out across the property and given such sophisticated names as Falmouth Avenue, Marblehead Road, Newport Avenue and Bar Harbor Road. A few of these lanes still survive as unpaved driveways leading north from Powder Point Avenue. The Park did not pan out and around 1905, Eben and Grace Ellison purchased a large portion of the land and built their summer home. With a permanent residence in Newton, Eben Ellison was a founder of Proctor & Ellison Co., a tanning business. The Powder Point estate, as shown here, was actively farmed well into the 20th century.

160 Powder Point Avenue   The Ellison Family retained the property until 1995. The view from Powder Point Avenue across the expansive grounds is striking to this day and all the more valuable when one considers that the same scene might have contained hundreds of cottages had things gone differently.

111

St. George &
Cedar Streets, c. 1880

At far right in this early view is the point where St. George and Cedar Streets split, both heading eastward. The fashionable Greek Revival house on the right was built by Charles H. Thomas, a merchant, in 1829. In 1864, his wife sold the house to Stephen Nye Gifford (1815-1886), long-time Clerk of the Massachusetts State Senate. Gifford would summer in Duxbury for the next two decades and became one of its most prominent citizens. His daughter, Mary Nye Gifford, would live in Duxbury most of her life, was Treasurer of the Rural and Historical Society for 59 years and, in her day, was known as the authority on local history. The date of construction of the Cape at left is unknown. Around the time this photograph was taken, it belonged to William Turner, a ships carpenter.

80 St. George Street & 4 Cedar Street

The same view shown in the historical photograph is impossible to obtain today due to the growth of trees. A closer view from St. George Street shows that the Gifford House has changed very little. The Cape has seen considerable changes since the late 19th century.

Bennett's Store, c. 1960

In the heart of the Island Creek neighborhood, this building, as with so many of Duxbury's stores, is older than it appears. It was originally a barn, built around 1890 or possibly earlier. It was converted into a store in the early 20th century and was purchased in 1940 by Arthur W. Bennett. The store contained a post office which served Island Creek and the Miramar Seminary on Parks Street. Bennett was postmaster from 1941 until 1968 when the post office closed. Arthur W. Bennett, Jr. bought the business from his father in 1968.

Bennett's Store,
136 Tremont Street

The Bennett family sold the store in 1982, however it continues to be known as "Bennett's" and is now a venerable landmark in a rapidly changing neighborhood.

115

Duxbury Yacht Club,
c. 1930

The Duxbury Yacht Club was organized in 1876. Its original clubhouse stood at the end of
Long Point Lane where Winsor's wharves had once been. In 1882, the organization occupied a
clubhouse on the pier of the Myles Standish Hotel on Standish shore, then in 1896 they built
a third clubhouse at the end of Freeman Place which still stands as a garage. Their fourth clubhouse,
depicted here, was constructed in 1913 at the end of Mattakeesett Court and is still in use today.

Duxbury Yacht Club, 23 Mattakeesett Court

The wooden bulkheads have since been replaced by cement. The new bulkhead along the town parking lot was placed significantly further back than the first. Despite these minor alterations to the shoreline, the view remains remarkably similar. The clubhouse itself is virtually unchanged. The two houses in the background still stand, although trees now obscure the Victorian house at 19 Long Point Lane. The white 1831 George Frazar House still overlooks the grassy site of the original 1876 clubhouse.

**Herrick's Auto Sales,
Tremont Street,
c. 1920**

Thomas Waldo Herrick (b. 1889) constructed this auto garage and dealership on Tremont Street around 1914. The service station was well placed to take advantage of the new influx of automobile tourists enjoying day trips from Boston down today's Route 3A.

118

*Holy Family Church
Parking Lot,
601 Tremont Street*

Herrick's old garage had fallen into disrepair by the 1980's and was razed to make way for the new Holy Family Church which was completed in 1988.

Snug Harbor,
c. 1965

In the early 19th century, much of this area was owned by shipbuilder Seth Sprague whose shipyard was to the left and whose wharf stood behind the present-day Snug Harbor Post Office. In the late 19th century, the area was dominated by W.S. Freeman's (now Sweetser's) general store (at left). It wasn't until the 1930's, however, that the area began to bloom as a business district. As it became a distinct neighborhood, it needed a name, and it was about that time that people began to refer to the vicinity as Snug Harbor. Just out of view to the right, as proclaimed by the sign, was Mike Butler's Snug Harbor Motors. The Village Pharmacy at right was run by Joe and Lydia Brandt. At center is the building that had been well known in the 1930's and 40's as the Snug Harbor Restaurant run by Arthur Murphy.

Snug Harbor   The district has changed very little since the 1960's, although the business names have changed. Snug Harbor Motors is now Expressions Pottery Studio. The Village Pharmacy is now Bayside Marine. Talbot's has since occupied the Snug Harbor Restaurant.

Powder Point Avenue, c. 1895

The area shown here, during the early to mid 19th century, was primarily the domain of the Drew Family. Duxbury's second most successful shipbuilding firm (outdone only by Ezra Weston II "King Caesar"), their patriarch was Sylvanus Drew (1735-1829) who began building vessels here in the late 1780's. His sons Charles and Reuben Drew took over the firm around 1800. Their shipyard was along the east side of Old Cove Street (just off the right side of this photograph) and their ships were launched across Powder Point Avenue into the Bluefish River. They built roughly 45 vessels until their firm collapsed during the depression following the Panic of 1837. By the time this photograph was taken, the Drew firm had been gone more than 50 years. The crumbling remains of their wharf are visible at right.

Powder Point Avenue
from 44 River Lane

This block along Powder Point Avenue has endured the years surprisingly well. All the houses shown in the historical photograph still stand, their facades virtually unchanged, each of them splendid examples of Federal architecture. Although barely discernable in the present day photograph, the stunted remains of the Drew wharf are still there amidst the marsh grass.

123

Island Creek, Tremont & Parks Streets, c. 1900

124

Since the 17th century, this intersection has been the center of what was then referred to as the Island Creek Settlement. Island Creek itself flows nearby into Kingston Bay. At its mouth is a small island—hence the name. Parks Street (running off to the right) and Oak Street (present but masked by trees to the left) were part of the 1623 Green Harbor Path running from Plymouth to Marshfield. Tremont Street was laid out in the 18th century, completing the intersection. At right is the Island Creek School, constructed in 1876. To the left of that is the 1896 Edgar F. Loring House at 155 Tremont Street and, left of that, is the c. 1853 Nathan Burgess III House at 167 Tremont Street. At far left is the barn that would one day become Bennett's Store.

Island Creek,
by 127 Tremont Street

The view is dramatically different today. No longer a rustic village, Island Creek is now a growing business district. During the 20th century, the prominent jog in Tremont Street was straightened. The Island Creek School was moved in the 1940's, deposited next to what was then Duxbury High School (now the Duxbury Free Library) and used for Home Economics classes. It eventually fell out of use and was razed when the library took over the property in 1997. The houses behind the site of the Island Creek School are still present at the aforementioned addresses, but hidden by trees in the present view.

125

ST. MARGURITE GIRLS HOME, SO. DUXBURY MASS. 3

St. Margaret's Girls Home,
c. 1915

In 1903, the Society of St. Margaret, an Episcopalian religious order, purchased 13 acres on Harden Hill in Duxbury to be used as a summer retreat by the sisters who resided in Boston. The land they purchased included the old shipyard that had belonged to Ezra Weston II at the foot of Harden Hill Lane—although by the time they bought it, little remained of the shipyard aside from a few outbuildings. In 1912, the Society began an "industrial summer school" for girls and built the building shown here to house them. It was named Bertram House after the principal benefactor of the project.

Bertram House,
St. Margaret's Convent,
21 Harden Hill Road

Today, Bertram House is still used as a retreat and conference center by various community and private groups. The area in the foreground is a portion of what is now known as Duxbury's Millennium Town Green. Purchased by the Town of Duxbury in 2000, the acquisition was made possible through a community fundraising effort jointly organized by the Town of Duxbury and the Wildlands Trust.

Congregational Church, DUXBURY, Mass.

Pilgrim Church &
St. John's Church,
Washington Street,
c. 1910

The two church buildings depicted here were both funded, for the most part, by shipbuilder Seth Sprague and built on land he donated. The first, now the Episcopalian Church of St. John the Evangelist, originally housed a Methodist congregation. Sprague sponsored the establishment of the church and was its most prominent member in 1823. An ardent antislavery activist, Sprague grew angry when the Methodist Church at large refused to denounce slavery. It is said a furious Sprague nailed his pew shut and stormed out of the church in the middle of a sermon. He then funded, in 1844, a Wesleyan Methodist church shown in the foreground that took a firm stance against slavery. It would seem, given the placement of the new church, that Sprague intended to literally eclipse the older church that had so incensed him.

**Pilgrim Church,
404 Washington Street**

The congregation of the new church officially transitioned from Wesleyan Methodist to Congregationalist in 1870 and is now known as the Pilgrim Church of Duxbury. The clock in the church steeple was given to the Town of Duxbury in memory of Almeda Ellison by her descendants. In 1905 it was decided during a Town Meeting that the best location for it would be Pilgrim Church. The steeple itself was modified in the 1950's. On the spot once occupied by old carriage sheds now stands the church hall added in 1956.

WASHINGTON ST. DUXBURY MASS.

Washington Street,
c. 1905

The building at left is the c. 1805 Stephen Churchill House at 332 Washington Street, built by a cooper. The next house is the 1803 Ahira Wadsworth House at 338 Washington Street. A sea captain and merchant, Wadsworth apparently had high taste. The house features delicate interior carvings unusual for Duxbury. Wadsworth went bankrupt in 1827 and the house was sold to Captain Martin Waterman. Waterman was one of the most respected of the captains who served Ezra Weston II "King Caesar." Four decades after Waterman purchased the house, the widow of Ahira Wadsworth announced that she had never relinquished her dower rights and sued the widow of Martin Waterman for possession of the estate. The house was divided down the middle and owned separately for a short time by the two widows. The next visible structure is the Village School, Duxbury's first two-room Grammar School constructed in 1902.

Washington Street & Stetson Place

The verandah on the Churchill House at left, a late Victorian embellishment, has since been removed. For much of the 20th century, the residence was known as the Dr. George Starr House. Starr purchased the property in the late 1940's. A physician and author, he was also an avid collector of rare duck decoys and possessed one of the largest such collections in the country. The Village School at the corner of Stetson Lane and Washington Street represented the Town's first departure from the system of one-room school houses and was hard-won point of pride for the School Committee. It served the Town well but was eventually replaced by new schools. Today, a newer house which bears some resemblance to the school occupies its site at 346 Washington Street.

131

Old Weston Mill, c. 1895

The millpond here depicted is one of the oldest man-made features in Duxbury. It was first created when William Hiller built a gristmill here in 1639. Later, the milldam and pond served the Weston Mill, lurking in the background of this photograph. Built in 1812, the mill was first used to make sailcloth for the firm of "King Caesar," then was later owned by the Ford family and produced textiles. By the time this photograph was taken, the mill had fallen out of use.

133

Millpond off Tremont Street

This view, facing east towards Tremont Street, shows the millpond still present. However the old Weston Mill burned to the ground around 1900, a victim of over-zealous youths who wanted to create Duxbury's largest Fourth of July bonfire. Although masked, Tremont Street runs just beyond the water's edge. The power lines running along side the street are just visible.

Paul Peterson's Drug Store, c. 1915

Around 1900, Nelson Stetson was the first to open a drugstore in the building at left. In 1907 he sold the store to 24 year-old Paul C. Peterson who ran it successfully for many years. At far right is the Duxbury Village Post Office, which was built about 1909 to replace its tiny neighbor, the building now known as the Bos'n's Locker, which had served as the Post Office since 1850. The Bos'n's Locker itself, looking rather dark, is visible to the left of the Post Office.

Washington Street near Fort Hill Lane

Peterson's Drug Store was a local landmark for decades. Even into the late 20th century, the building was still an antiques store and has only recently been fully converted into a residence. The old Post Office at right in the historical photograph, was moved in the 1940's to 64 Standish Street and the present, similar house built on its site.

135

Clapp Laboratories & Snug Harbor, 1946

Another aerial view taken for the William F. Clapp Laboratories (now owned by the Battelle Institute), the grounds of the labs are just right of center. Also depicted is the Pilgrim Church, which did not receive its spire until the 1950's.

Snug Harbor   The towering spires of Pilgrim Church (left) and the Church of St. John the Evangelist (right) are the only structures along Washington Street that are clearly visible above today's foliage. Along the waterfront, Bayside Marine makes for a dramatic addition to the landscape, occupying the marsh flats at lower right in the historical photograph. The ship docked at the Duxbury Bay Maritime School is the *Friendship* of Salem, a replica of a 1797 merchant vessel. Her visit to Duxbury was part of the DBMS's Opening of the Bay celebration in 2008. The ship's size and configuration are quite similar to vessels once launched from Duxbury's shores. The remains of one of Winsor's wharves is visible at lower right.

137

A. R. PARKER CO.
DAIRY STATION
AT DUXBURY, MASS.
Off Route 3

DUXBURY

◆

AT the Tree of Knowledge, a hollow tree in which the post runner deposited mail in his horseback journeys between Plymouth and Massachusetts Bay Colonies.

A.R. Parker Dairy Station, c. 1930

Located at the Tree of Knowledge Corner, the Parker dairy station was an outlet for the dairy items produced at the family's farm in Bridgewater. The corner, as the advertisement indicates, took its name from an old tree that stood on the site in the late 18th and early 19th centuries. The mail left there by post riders and stage coach drivers from Boston brought all manner of news from beyond Duxbury, and so the tree came to be known as the Tree of Knowledge. According to tradition, in the early 19th century when the tree began to die, an elderly resident dreamt that the tree spoke to him, stating that Duxbury would be cursed should the tree ever be forgotten. The location has therefore been marked ever since by various painted signs, and now a granite marker.

Tree of Knowledge Corner

Today's Elm, Summer and South Streets meet at the location where colonial post riders once deposited mail for Duxbury residents. The exact location of the Parker Dairy Station is not known for certain, however the land in the background that now contains houses, was owned by A. R. Parker and it is believed that the quaint road stand stood near Elm Street to the left of this photograph.

139

Fourth of July Parade,
Snug Harbor, c. 1950

One of Duxbury's curious traditions during the 20th century, the "Horribles" were elaborate floats and bizarre, modified automobiles constructed annually for the Fourth of July Parade. A prize awaited the team that built the most outlandish Horrible. An early example can be seen at center—a stripped-down old Ford with a banner proclaiming it, "The Car of the Year." Eventually, the Horribles began to push the limits of good taste, according to many, and were discontinued around 1980. Still, mere mention of the Horribles brings a smile to the faces of those who remember them. The building at right in the photograph is Sprague Hall, a meeting place for many community organizations. It was moved and is now a residence at 9 Beaverbrook Lane.

Snug Harbor   Aside from the shifting of Sprague Hall, very little has changed along this portion of Washington Street since the mid 20th century.

141

Cook House, c. 1910   This house was built c. 1871 by George B. Prior. The owner around the time this photograph was taken was Willard R. Cook, a blacksmith. A widower, he resided here with his son, daughter, a boarder and a housekeeper.

35 Standish Street   Today, the house is remarkably well preserved. Even the tree visible in the historic photograph is still living—a behemoth in the present day view.

143

Lydia Keene Farm,
_c. 1920_

At the time of this photograph, the Keene Farm near the corner of Keene and Temple Streets was owned by Lydia Keene. The property had belonged to her family for generations. Her father, Isaac Keene, a farmer, owned it for much of the 19th century. The exact age of the building has not yet been determined, however it likely dates to the 18th century. The Keene family has a long history in that area of Duxbury, beginning with Josiah Keene who was granted land nearby in 1700 and built a sawmill along what became known as Keene's Brook.

Camp Wing,
742 Keene Street

The barn and house still stand. According to tradition, the barn is the biggest in Duxbury. The property is today part of Camp Wing, a retreat for youths operated by Crossroads for Kids, Inc. of Boston. In 1998, the Town of Duxbury purchased 354 acres of the Camp Wing property to be preserved as conservation land.

145

St. George Hotel
St. George Hotel, Washington Street, c. 1910

In 1890, according to author Margery MacMillan, George and Louise Scott purchased this house at the corner of Washington Street and Sunset Road. They opened an inn and restaurant there and thus became, in all likelihood, the first African-American business owners in Duxbury. The restaurant was highly regarded and quite busy, hosting banquets for community organizations.

576 Washington Street   In 1926, the hotel was purchased by William Way and renamed the Way Croft Inn. Its popularity continued and the building was gradually enlarged to accommodate more guests. Today it is a private residence.

View from the
Church of St. John the Evangelist,
c. 1900

This extraordinary view depicts a congregation leaving the Church of St. John the Evangelist. The church itself was at the photographer's back and so is not visible. It had originally been built as a Methodist Meeting House in 1823, however the Methodists vacated the building in the mid 19th century and the church sat vacant for many years. It was eventually purchased by Lucy Sprague Sampson in 1894 for the community's new Episcopalian congregation. The building was consecrated in 1900 and it is possible that this photograph was taken on that occasion. Alternatively, it may also have been taken after a special Memorial Day service given the number of Civil War Veterans in uniform in the foreground. Pilgrim Church, lacking its 20th century additions, is stands prominently atop the hill right of center. To the right of that is the building now known as the Winsor House Inn.

**View from the
Church of St. John the Evangelist,
410 Washington Street**

Time has dramatically altered the landscape of this hillside that is home to two churches. The only recognizable feature in the same view today is the spire of Pilgrim Church, visible through a convenient gap in the trees.

employed in commerce and the fisheries. There are 4 churches, 2 Methodist, 1 Unitarian, and 1 Universalist. Population, 2,789. Distance, 6 miles north of Plymouth, and 29 south-east of Boston.

South-western view of Duxbury.

The above shows the appearance of Duxbury as it is entered from the south-west. The village is mostly built on a single street, about two miles in length, and consists of upwards of 100 dwelling-houses, situated on a gentle and somewhat of a sandy elevation, above the sea. *Blue-fish* river crosses th... part of the village ...

"South-western view of Duxbury," 1839

This sketch, rendered just at the dawn of photography, is the oldest image in this publication. It depicts two travelers strolling northward along what is now known as Washington Street. The utterly treeless landscape was probably accurate. Most of New England was deforested in the 19th century as trees were felled for firewood and building material. The church spire in the distance belongs to the building presently occupied by the Church of St. John the Evangelist, built in 1823 and originally a Methodist Meeting House. The image was drawn for an 1839 County Atlas. According to the publication, Duxbury was "mostly built on a single street, about two miles in length, and consists of upwards of 100 dwelling houses, situated on a gentle and somewhat of a sandy elevation above the sea. Blue-fish River crosses the road in the northern part of the village, at which place most of the ship-building done in the village is carried on."

View from the Town Green, Washington Street

The same view today does not provide any such panorama of Duxbury Village due to the growth of trees over the course of the 20th century. The photograph was taken looking northeast from the Town Green on Washington Street just outside of Hall's Corner, the approximate location from which the sketch was rendered. The two pedestrians strolled by out of sheer coincidence... a curious echo from the past.

151

Sources

"150th Anniversary Program, Corner Stone Lodge, A.F. & A.M.," Drew Archives of the Duxbury Rural and Historical Society.

"New Retail Offices at Cox's Corner," *Duxbury Clipper*, August 9, 1989.

"The History of the Pilgrim Church." Pilgrim Church vertical file, Drew Archives of the Duxbury Rural and Historical Society. June 14, 1956.

Browne, Patrick T.J. "Joseph Soule House." Dateboard files, Drew Archives of the Duxbury Rural and Historical Society. 2008.

Browne, Patrick T.J. *King Caesar of Duxbury: Exploring the World of Ezra Weston, Shipbuilder and Merchant*. Duxbury: Duxbury Rural and Historical Society, 2006.

Browne, Patrick T.J. "Winfield Scott Freeman House." Dateboard files, Drew Archives of the Duxbury Rural and Historical Society. 2004.

Davis, Karen. "35 Standish Street," *Duxbury Community Survey*, v. 2. Drew Archives of the Duxbury Rural and Historical Society. Unpublished Report to the Duxbury Historical Commission, 2001.

Davis, Karen. "Eben and Grace Ellison House, 160 Powder Point Avenue," *Duxbury Community Survey*, v. 3. Drew Archives of the Duxbury Rural and Historical Society. Unpublished Report to the Duxbury Historical Commission, 2004.

Davis, Karen. "Hall's Corner Historical Narrative," *Duxbury Community Survey*, v. 2. Drew Archives of the Duxbury Rural and Historical Society. Unpublished Report to the Duxbury Historical Commission, 2001.

Davis, Karen. "Josephus Dawes House, 158 Tremont Street," *Duxbury Community Survey*, v. 3. Drew Archives of the Duxbury Rural and Historical Society. Unpublished Report to the Duxbury Historical Commission, 2001.

Davis, Karen. "Myron M. White House, 38 Standish Street" *Duxbury Community Survey*, v. 2. Drew Archives of the Duxbury Rural and Historical Society. Unpublished Report to the Duxbury Historical Commission, 2001.

Davis, Karen. "Stephen Churchill House, 332 Washington Street," *Duxbury Community Survey*, v. 1. Drew Archives of the Duxbury Rural and Historical Society. Unpublished Report to the Duxbury Historical Commission, 2001.

Dente, Robert. "Dr. Nathaniel Kingsbury Noyes House." Dateboard files, Drew Archives of the Duxbury Rural and Historical Society. 1998.

Dente, Robert. "William Martin Brewster House." Dateboard files, Drew Archives of the Duxbury Rural and Historical Society. 2007.

Ford, John Jr. "Map of Duxbury, Mass." 1833

Forgit, Norman R. *Duxbury… An Album*. Duxbury: Duxbury Rural and Historical Society, 2004.

Gardener, George. "Thomas Delano House." Dateboard files, Drew Archives of the Duxbury Rural and Historical Society. 1968.

Goodrich, Benjamin F., et. al., "Report of the Building Committee of the New High School," *Annual Report of the Town Officers and Committees of the Town of Duxbury for the Year Ending Dec. 31st 1927*. Plymouth: The Rogers Print, 1928.

Kelso, Tony. "The Lives of 9 and 8 Standish Street," *Duxbury Clipper*, April 7, 2004

Kelso, Tony. "Benjamin Freeman House," Dateboard files, Drew Archives of the Duxbury Rural and Historical Society. 1991.

Love, Sarah. "Bridge Spans 100 Years," *Duxbury Reporter*, October 14, 1992.

MacMillan, Margery. *Stopping Places Along Duxbury Roads*. Duxbury: Duxbury Rural and Historical Society, 1991.

Merry, Harriet H. "St. Margaret's Convent in Duxbury." St. Margaret's vertical file, Drew Archives of the Duxbury Rural and Historical Society.

Mittell, David A. *The Duxbury Yacht Club Story*. Attleborough: Colonial Lithograph, 1995.

Peterson, Elizabeth. "The Ladies of Duxbury Hall." 1960. Printed in the *Duxbury Clipper*, January 20, 1993.

Pillsbury, Katherine H. *Duxbury… A Guide*. Duxbury: Duxbury Rural and Historical Society, 1999.

ed. Pillsbury, Katherine H; Hale, Robert D; Post, Jack. *The Duxbury Book 1637-1987*. Duxbury: Duxbury Rural and Historical Society

Richards, L.J. & Co. *New Topographical Atlas of Surveys, Plymouth County*. Springfield: L.J. Richards & Co., 1903.

Seaver, Virginia. "Charles C. Cochs House." Dateboard files, Drew Archives of the Duxbury Rural and Historical Society

Seaver, Virginia. "Joseph Prior House." Dateboard files, Drew Archives of the Duxbury Rural and Historical Society. 1978.

Soule, Nathan T., et. al., "School Report," *Annual Report of the Town Officers and Committees of the Town of Duxbury for the Year Ending January 1, 1903*. Plymouth: The Memorial Press, 1903.

Walker, George H. *Atlas of Plymouth County, Massachusetts*. Boston: George H. Walker & Co., 1879.

Walling, Henry F. *Map of the County of Plymouth Massachusetts*. Boston: D.R. Smith, 1857.

Wentworth, Dorothy. "Ahira Wadsworth House." Dateboard files, Drew Archives of the Duxbury Rural and Historical Society

Wentworth, Dorothy. *Settlement and Growth of Duxbury 1628-1870*. Duxbury: Duxbury Rural and Historical Society, 1973.

Wentworth, Dorothy. *The Alden Family in the Alden House*. Duxbury: Duxbury Rural and Historical Society, 1980.

Winsor, Justin. *History of the Town of Duxbury*. Boston: Crosby & Nichols, 1849.

Index